SPORTS MVPs

SHOHEI OHTANI

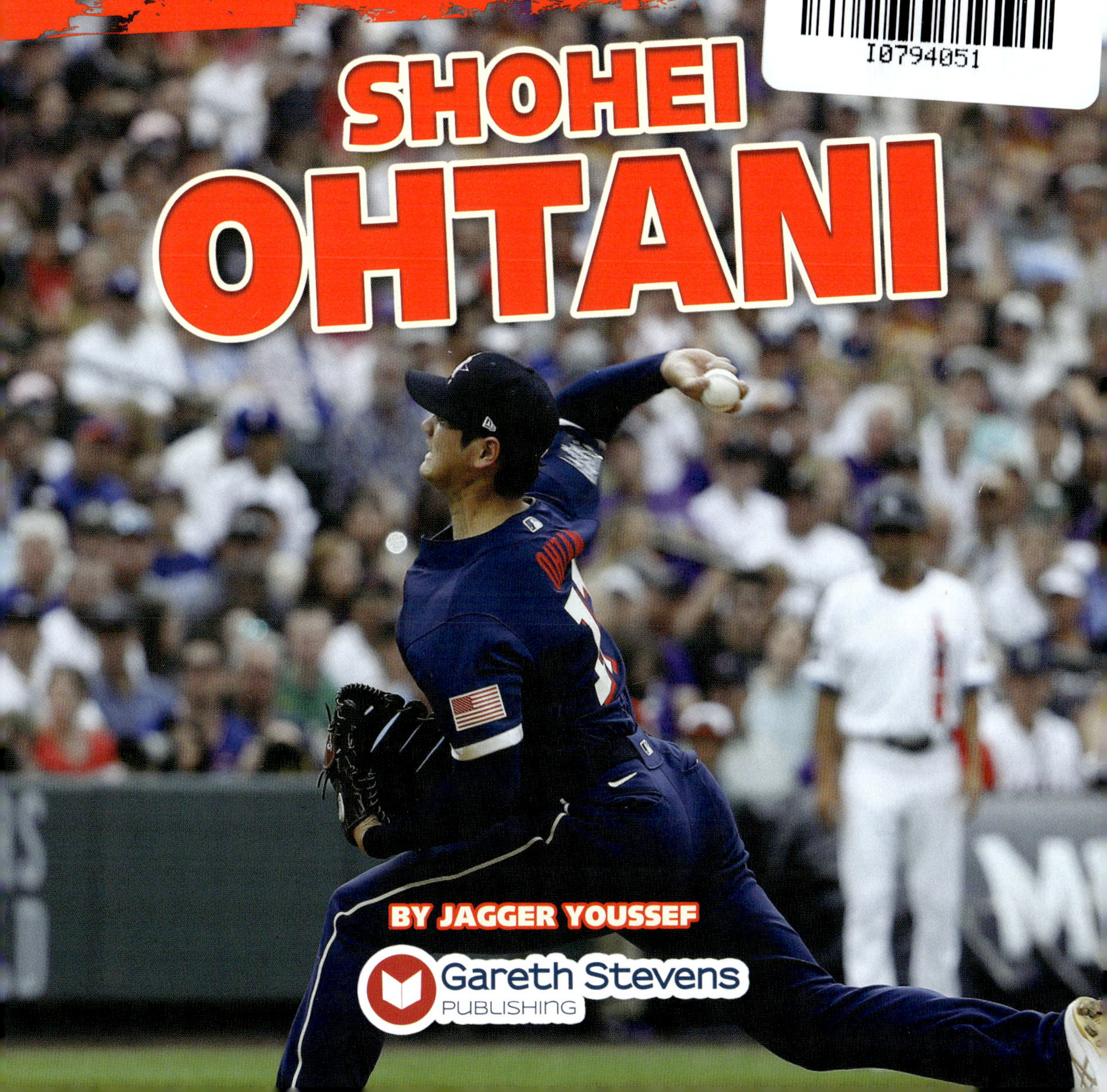

BY JAGGER YOUSSEF

Gareth Stevens PUBLISHING

Please visit our website, www.garethstevens.com. For a free color catalog of all our high-quality books, call toll free 1-800-542-2595 or fax 1-877-542-2596.

Library of Congress Cataloging-in-Publication Data

Names: Youssef, Jagger, author.
Title: Shohei Ohtani / Jagger Youssef.
Description: New York : Gareth Stevens Publishing, [2024] | Series: Sports MVPs | Includes index.
Identifiers: LCCN 2023009530 (print) | LCCN 2023009531 (ebook) | ISBN 9781538285879 (library binding) | ISBN 9781538285862 (paperback) | ISBN 9781538285886 (ebook)
Subjects: LCSH: Ohtani, Shohei, 1994—Juvenile literature. | Pitchers (Baseball)–United States–Biography–Juvenile literature. | Pitchers (Baseball)–Japan–Biography–Juvenile literature. | California Angels (Baseball team)–History–Juvenile literature.
Classification: LCC GV865.O42 Y6 2024 (print) | LCC GV865.O42 (ebook) | DDC 796.357092 [B]–dc23/eng/20230306
LC record available at https://lccn.loc.gov/2023009530
LC ebook record available at https://lccn.loc.gov/2023009531

Published in 2024 by
Gareth Stevens Publishing
2544 Clinton St,
Buffalo, NY 14224

Designer: Claire Wrazin
Editor: Therese Shea

Photo credits: Cover, pp. 1, 17 UPI/Alamy Stock Photo; pp. 5, 13, 15, 19 Conor P. Fitzgerald/Shutterstock.com; p. 7 REUTERS/Alamy Stock Photo; p. 9 File:Shohei_Ohtani_pitching_2013.03.10_(8543818939).jpg/Wikimedia Commons; p. 11 KYDPL KYODO/Associated Press; p. 21 File:Shohei_Ohtani_(52251828753).jpg/Wikimedia Commons.

Printed in the United States of America

CPSIA compliance information: Batch #CS24GS: For further information contact Gareth Stevens, New York, New York at 1-800-542-2595.

CONTENTS

It's Shotime! 4

Baseball Brothers 6

A Fighter 8

Into MLB. 12

All-Star 16

Legend in the Making 20

Glossary. 22

For More Information. 23

Index 24

Boldface words appear in the glossary.

It's Shotime!

Shohei Ohtani (SHO-hay oh-TAH-nee) is a baseball star. His **nickname** is "Shotime." He puts on an amazing "show" for fans! Shohei is a great pitcher and a great batter too. He also had one of the fastest runs to first base during 2022—4.09 seconds!

ANGELS

Baseball Brothers

Shohei Ohtani was born July 5, 1994, in Oshu, Japan. Shohei and his brother, Ryuta, began playing baseball at a young age. By the time Shohei was 17, he could throw the ball 99 miles (159 km) per hour!

A Fighter

In 2012, Shohei was the first pick in the Nippon Professional Baseball (NPB) **draft**. The NPB is the highest pro **league** in Japan. He was chosen by a team called the Hokkaido Nippon-Ham Fighters. They promised he could pitch and bat.

Shohei became stronger in the NPB. He pitched and played in the **outfield**. He began hitting powerful home runs. In 2015 and 2016, he had the best **ERA**. In 2016, the Fighters won the Pacific League and Japan Series **championships**.

HOKKAIDO
NIPPONHAM

Into MLB

In 2017, Shohei made the jump to Major League Baseball (MLB). He signed with the Los Angeles Angels. Pitchers in MLB are usually poor batters. But Shohei is a true "two-way player." He can pitch well and bat well.

NGELS

In Shohei's first year, he was named the American League's **Rookie** of the Year. But he struggled in 2019 and 2020 because of **injuries**. In 2021, he hit 46 home runs and had 100 runs batted in (RBIs). As a starting pitcher, he threw 156 strikeouts.

ANGELS
17

All-Star

Shohei was named an All-Star in 2021 for both his positions: pitcher and **designated hitter**. He was the first player in MLB history to receive this honor. He was also named the American League's Most Valuable Player (MVP).

Shohei's 2022 season was just as amazing. He had an ERA of 2.33 in 28 starts. He threw 219 strikeouts. As a designated hitter, he had 34 home runs and 95 RBIs. Again, he was named a designated hitter All-Star and starting pitcher All-Star.

Legend in the Making

Many baseball fans think Shohei is one of the best baseball players ever. He turned down a national honor in Japan because he says he has much more to accomplish. What records will the two-way wonder break next?

MORE TO KNOW

Shohei is a right-handed pitcher and a left-handed batter.

Shohei is 6 feet 4 inches (193 cm) tall.

Shohei's jersey number is 17.

Shohei likes playing video games.

Shohei has two Guinness World Records for MLB.

GLOSSARY

championship: A contest to decide an overall winner.

designated hitter: A player who is chosen at the start of a game to bat in the place of the pitcher.

draft: The act of picking players for a team.

ERA: Earned run average, which is the number of earned runs allowed against the pitcher divided by innings pitched multiplied by nine.

injury: Harm or damage to the body.

league: A group of sports teams that face each other.

nickname: A name different from a real name that people call someone when they are talking to or about them.

outfield: The area beyond the infield and between the foul lines.

rookie: A first-year player in a professional sport.

FOR MORE INFORMATION

BOOKS

Downs, Kieran. *Shohei Ohtani.* Minneapolis, MN: Bellwether Media, 2023.

Fishman, Jon M. *Shohei Ohtani.* Minneapolis, MN: Lerner Publications, 2022.

Kim, Cheryl. *Shohei Ohtani: Baseball Trailblazer.* North Mankato, MN: Capstone Press, 2024

WEBSITES

Shohei Ohtani Facts for Kids
kids.kiddle.co/Shohei_Ohtani#
Read about more records this two-way player has broken.

Shohei Ohtani #17
www.mlb.com/player/shohei-ohtani-660271
This player page has all the stats about Shohei.

Publisher's note to educators and parents: Our editors have carefully reviewed these websites to ensure that they are suitable for students. Many websites change frequently, however, and we cannot guarantee that a site's future contents will continue to meet our high standards of quality and educational value. Be advised that students should be closely supervised whenever they access the internet.

INDEX

designed hitter, 16, 18

ERA, 10, 18

Hokkaido Nippon-Ham Fighters, 8, 10

home runs, 10, 14, 18

Japan, 6, 8, 10, 20

Los Angeles Angels, 12

Major League Baseball (MLB), 12, 16, 21

Most Valuable Player (MVP), 16

Nippon Professional Baseball (NPB), 8, 10

pitcher, 4, 12, 14, 18, 21

Rookie of the Year, 14

Ryuta, 6